MUHAMMAD
The Messenger of Allah

PERSECUTION & HIJRA

In the name of Allah the Most Beneficent, Most Merciful

ح) المكتب التعاوني للدعوة والإرشاد و توعية الجاليات بالربوة، ١٤٣٨هـ
فهرسة مكتبة الملك فهد الوطنية أثناء النشر

مركز أصول العالمي
سلسلة كتيبات التعريف بالنبي محمد رسول الله - اللغة الإنجليزية. /
مركز أصول العالمي. - الرياض، ١٤٣٩هـ
٣٦ ص، ١١,٥ سم ١٥ x سم

ردمك : ٣-٠٩-٨٢٤٩-٦٠٣-٩٧٨ (مجموعة)
٧-١١-٨٢٤٩-٦٠٣-٩٧٨ (ج٢)

١- السيرة النبوية   أ. العنوان
ديوي ٢٣٩   ١٤٣٩/٨٨٤٤

رقم الإيداع: ١٤٣٩/٨٨٤٤

ردمك : ٣-٠٩-٨٢٤٩-٦٠٣-٩٧٨ (مجموعة)
٧-١١-٨٢٤٩-٦٠٣-٩٧٨ (ج٢)

MUHAMMAD
The Messenger of Allah

PERSECUTION & HIJRA

Terms

Terminology used in this series of booklets.
(Taken from Sheikh Mahmoud Murad's book, *Common Mistakes in Translation*).

Rubb: Some prefer to translate the term "Rubb" into "Lord". Beside the fact that the latter is a Biblical term referring to the alleged lordship of the servant of God, the Prophet Jesus, the word lord, which is limited to mean: master, chief, proprietor, or ruler, can never convey the conclusive significance of the term "Rubb". Among other meanings, the term "Rubb" means: the Creator, the Fashioner, the Provider, the One upon Whom all creatures depend for their means of subsistence, and the One Who gives life and causes death.

Deen: The word translated as religion is "Deen", which in Arabic commonly refers to a way of life, which is both private and public. It is an inclusive term meaning: acts of worship, political practice, and a detailed code of conduct, including hygiene or etiquette matters.

Sal'lal'laahu a'laihi wa sal'lam **:** This Arabic term means, "may God praise him and render him safe from all evil."

BOOKLET 2

This book is the second in a series of publications based on a book titled *Muhammad, the Messenger of Allah*. Each booklet covers an aspect of the Prophet's life, deeds and teachings, and aims to provide a better understanding of Islam.

INTRODUCTION

All praise is due to Allah, the Rubb of the two worlds, and may Allah exalt the mention of his Prophet, and render him and his household safe and secure from all the derogatory things.

This booklet concentrates on the difficult times that faced Muhammad  and his few followers in Makkah at the start of the call to Islam.

This booklet shows that Quraish, who considered themselves the noblest tribe in the Arabian Peninsula, refused to accept that all people are equal, as is believed in the Deen of Islam. Furthermore, the Deen of Islam did not only call on them to worship Allah alone. It prohibited them from customs they used to practice in their life, things they considered pleasurable, such as fornication and gambling. The call of Muhammad told them that there was no difference between people except through piety.

But Quraish, who believed that they were the noblest tribe, wondered how the noblest tribe among the Arabs could stand to be treated equally with slaves. Thus, they adamantly refused to accept Islam. They harmed the Messenger of Allah and tortured his followers. They described him as crazy, a sorcerer and a liar.

This booklet also shows that the Prophet was not deterred by this harsh treatment. He went on preaching his call (Da'wah), and he met with tribes that used to come to Makkah for Hajj. In these meetings, he would invite them to embrace Islam. With Allah's help, a few people from Yathrib (later renamed Madinah) embraced Islam and invited the Prophet to come to their city and pledged to support him.

The Prophet ordered his

followers to migrate to Madinah, after all the hardships that the Muslims of Makkah faced at the hands of Quraish. Hence, Madinah became the capital of the fledgling Muslim state and the point from which the Da'wah spread.

As this booklet shows, the people of Madinah greatly loved the Prophet ﷺ more than they loved themselves. The Prophet ﷺ settled there and started teaching People the Quran and Islamic Jurisprudence. It was also from

From there the Messenger of Allah fought his first battle against Quraish, his own people who expelled him from Makkah.

When Quraish learned that the Da'wah of Islam was spreading rapidly from Madinah, they fought with the Prophet ﷺ at the Battle of Badr. The battle was unequal, as it took place between two unequal groups in both numbers and weaponry. The Muslims were only 314, whereas the enemy was 1000 strong. There, Allah gave the Prophet ﷺ and his Companions their first victory over the disbelievers.

MUHAMMAD The Messenger of Allah

there that the Messenger of Allah ﷺ fought his first battle against Quraish, his own people who expelled him from Makkah. That was the battle of Badr, in which he was victorious.

He continued to fight against the Quraish in various skirmishes, but it was only after 8 years that the Prophet ﷺ was able to prepare an army of 10,000 loyal soldiers and headed towards Makkah and conquered it without a battle or bloodshed. With this victory, he defeated his own people who had harmed him and tortured his companions in every way.

ولينصرنك الله نصراً عزيزاً

"And that Allah may aid you with a mighty victory." [48:3]

2

PERSECUTION AND HIJRA

The religion of Islam is a complete way of life, which deals with religious, political, economical and social affairs. Furthermore, the religion of Islam did not only call them to worship God alone and to forsake all idols rather, it prohibited them from things they considered pleasurable, such as consuming interest and intoxicants, fornication, and gambling.

It also called people to be just and fair with one another, and to know that there was no difference between them except through piety. How could the Quraish, the most noble tribe amongst the Arabs, stand to be treated equally with slaves! They did not only adamantly refuse to accept Islam, rather, they harmed him and blamed him, saying that he was crazy, a sorcerer and a liar. They ac-

MUHAMMAD The Messenger of Allah

• Muhammad

cused him of things they would never have dared to do before the advent of Islam. They incited the ignorant masses against him, harmed him and tortured his companions. Abdullah b. Masood, a close companion of the Prophet, reports:

"While the Prophet was standing up and praying near the Ka'bah, a group of Quraish were sitting nearby when one of them said, 'Do you see this man? Would someone bring the bloody intestines (removed after the slaughter) of the camels, and wait till he prostrates, and then dump it on his back?' The most wretched amongst them volunteered to do it, and when the Prophet prostrated, he poured the filth over his back, so the Prophet stayed in prostration. They laughed so hard that they were about to fall on each other. Someone went to Fatimah, the Prophet's daughter who was a young girl at the time, and informed

The Quraish did not only adamantly refuse to accept Islam, rather, they harmed him and blamed him, saying that Muhammad was crazy, a sorcerer and a liar.

2

her of what had happened. She hurriedly came towards the Prophet ﷺ and removed the filth from his back, and then she turned and cursed the Quraishites sitting nearby." *(Bukhari)*

Muneeb Al-Azdi, a companion of the Prophet ﷺ said:

"I saw the Messenger of God in the Era of Ignorance saying to people, 'Say there is nothing worthy of being worshipped except Allah if you desire success.' There were those who spat in his face, those who threw soil in his face, and those who swore at him until midday. Once, a young girl came with a big container of water offering it to him.

Muhammad ﷺ called the many tribes that came to Makkah for Hajj to Islam. A few believed from the people of Yathrib, which is known today as Madinah.

MUHAMMAD The Messenger of Allah

He washed his face and hands and said, 'O daughter, do not fear that your father will be humiliated or struck by poverty.'" *(Mu'jam Al-Kabeer)*

Abdullah b. Amr ibn Al-Aas, a companion of the Prophet ﷺ, was asked about some of the evil the pagans did to the Prophet ﷺ, to which he replied:

"Once a pagan approached the Prophet ﷺ while he was praying near the Ka'bah and twisted his garment around his neck. Abu-Bakr[1] hurriedly approached and grabbed his shoulder and pushed him away saying, 'Would you kill a man only because he proclaims Allah as his Lord, while clear signs have come to you from your Lord?'" *(Bukhari)*

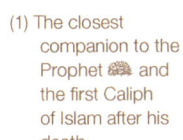

(1) The closest companion to the Prophet ﷺ and the first Caliph of Islam after his death.

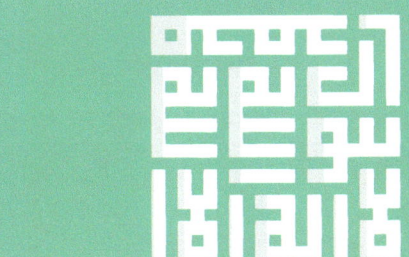

لا إله إلا الله
محمد رسول الله

There Is No God But Allah And Muhammad Is The Messenger Of God

2

The people of Madinah welcomed the new Muslim immigrants and received them in a most hospitable manner.

These incidents did not stop the Prophet ﷺ from calling to Islam. He preached this message to the many tribes that came to Makkah for Hajj[(1)]. A few believed from the people of Yathrib, a small city north of Makkah known today as Madinah, and they pledged to support him and help him if he chose to migrate there. He sent with them Mus'ab b. Umair to teach them the tenets of Islam. After all the hardships that the Muslims of Makkah faced from their own people, God granted them the permission to migrate to Madinah. The people of Madinah welcomed them and received them in a most hospitable manner. Madinah became the capital of the new Muslim state, and the place from which the call to Islam was spread far and wide.

The Prophet ﷺ settled there and taught people the Qur'an and the rulings of the religion. The inhabitants of Madinah were greatly moved and touched by the Prophet's manners. They loved him more than they loved their own selves. They would rush to serve him, and they would spend all they had in the path of Islam. The society was strong and its people were rich in Faith. People loved each other, and true brotherhood was apparent amongst its people. All people were equal - the rich and poor, the black and white, the Arab and non-Arab - all were considered as equals in the religion of God and no distinction was made among them except through piety.

After the Quraish learned that the

(1) Pilgrimage to Makkah.

2

The Prophet was able to prepare an army 10,000 strong. They headed towards Makkah and conquered it.

Prophet's call had spread, they fought him in the first battle in Islam, the Battle of Badr. The battle took place between two groups unequal in both numbers and weaponry. The Muslims were only 314, whereas the enemy was 1000 strong. There, Allah gave the Prophet and his Companions their first victory over the disbelievers. After this battle, a number of battles took place between the Muslims and the pagans. After eight years, the Prophet was able to prepare an army 10,000 strong. They proceeded towards Makkah and conquered it without spilling a drop of blood, and with this Muhamamad overcame the people who had harmed and tortured him and his Companions with every conceivable cruelty. The year of this decisive victory is called "The Year of the Conquest." Allah, the Exalted, says:

"When the victory of Allah has come and the conquest, and you see the people entering

MUHAMMAD The Messenger of Allah

• Muhammad

into the religion of Allah in multitudes, then repeat the praises of your Lord and ask forgiveness of Him. Indeed, He is ever Accepting of repentance." *[110:1-3]*

Upon the conquest, the Prophet gathered the people of Makkah and said to them:

"What do you think I will do to you?' They answered, 'You will only do something favorable. You are a kind and generous brother, and a kind and generous nephew!' The Prophet said, 'Go, for you are free.'" (Baihaqi)

This incredible act of forgiveness caused many to accept Islam. The Prophet then returned to Madinah. After a period of time, the Prophet intended to perform Hajj, so he headed towards Makkah with 114,000 Companions and performed Hajj. This Hajj is known as the "Farewell Pilgrimage" since the Prophet never performed another Hajj, and died shortly after he performed it.

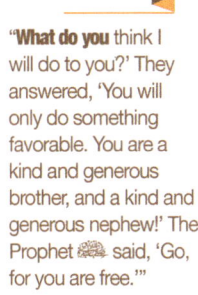

"**What do you** think I will do to you?' They answered, 'You will only do something favorable. You are a kind and generous brother, and a kind and generous nephew!' The Prophet said, 'Go, for you are free.'"

2

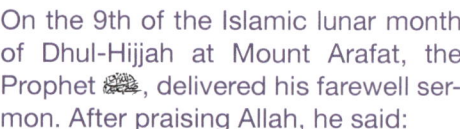

On the 9th of the Islamic lunar month of Dhul-Hijjah at Mount Arafat, the Prophet ﷺ, delivered his farewell sermon. After praising Allah, he said:

"O people! Lend me an attentive ear, for I know not whether after this year, I shall ever be amongst you again. Therefore, listen to what I am saying to you very carefully and take these words to those who could not be present here today.

O people! Just as you regard this month, this day, and this city as sacred, so regard the life and property of every Muslim. Return the goods entrusted to you to their rightful owners. Hurt no one so that no one may hurt you. Remember, you will indeed meet your Lord and He will

The Prophet ﷺ said, "You will neither inflict, nor suffer, inequity. Beware of Satan for the safety of your religion. He has lost all hope that he will ever be able to lead you astray in great things, so beware of following him in small things."

- Muhammad ﷺ

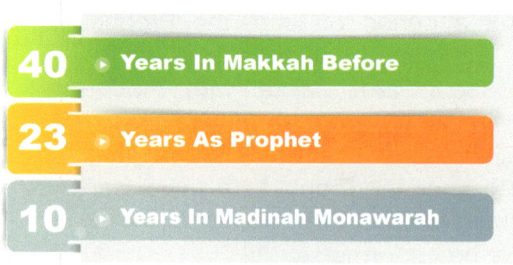

40 ▸ Years In Makkah Before

23 ▸ Years As Prophet

10 ▸ Years In Madinah Monawarah

indeed reckon your deeds. Allah has forbidden you to take usury. Therefore, all interest due shall henceforth be waived. Your capital, however, is yours to keep. You will neither inflict, nor suffer, inequity. Beware of Satan for the safety of your religion. He has lost all hope that he will ever be able to lead you astray in great things, so beware of following him in small things.

O people! It is true that you have certain rights with regards to your women, but they also have rights over you… If they abide by your right, then to them belongs the right of provisions and to be clothed in a good manner. Treat women well and be kind to them, for they are your partners. Remember that you have taken them as your wives only

(1) George Bernard Shaw, "A Shavian Meets a Theologian" Interview by M A A Siddiqui in "Genuine Islam", Organ of the Al-Malaya Missionary Society Vol 1, No 1, January, 1936 B Lib catalogue.

"I have studied this wonderful man [Muhammad], and in my opinion, far from being an anti-Christ, he must be called the Saviour of Humanity."[1]

under Allah's trust and with His permission.

O people! Listen to me in earnest. Worship Allah, perform your five daily prayers, fast the month of Ramadan, give alms and perform the pilgrimage (i.e. Hajj) if you can afford it. All mankind is from Adam and Adam is from clay. There is no superiority for an Arab over a non-Arab, nor for a non-Arab over an Arab, or for a white over a black, nor for a black over a white, except through piety. Know that every Muslim is a brother to every other Muslim and that the Muslims are one community. Nothing shall be legitimate to a Muslim that belongs to another, unless it was given freely and willingly. Do not, therefore, do injustice to yourselves.

Remember, one day you will appear before Allah and answer for your

MUHAMMAD The Messenger of Allah

deeds. So beware! Do not stray from the path of righteousness after I am gone. O people! No prophet or messenger will come after me, and no new faith will be born. Reason well, therefore, O people! And understand the words that I convey to you. I leave behind me two things, if you follow them you will never go astray: the Book of Allah (i.e. the Qur'an) and my Sunnah. All those who listen to me shall pass on my words to others, and those to others again. May the last ones understand my words better than those who listen to me directly. Be my witness, O Allah, that I have conveyed Your Message to Your people." (Collected from Bukhari, Muslim, Ahmad)

The Prophet died in Madinah in the year 632 C.E. and was buried there as well. The Prophet was 63 years of age when he died. The Muslims were shocked when they learned of his death; some Companions could not even believe it. Abu-

Bakr then addressed the Muslims and read the words of God:

"Muhammad is not but a messenger. Other messengers have passed on before him. So if he was to die or be killed, would you turn back on your heels to unbelief? And he who turns back on his heels will never harm Allah at all. But Allah will reward the grateful." [3:144]

When the believers heard this verse, they were reminded of the truth and quickly controlled their extreme sorrow, just as the Prophet ﷺ had taught them.

The Prophet ﷺ stayed in Makkah for forty years before being commissioned as a Prophet. After being commissioned as a Prophet, he lived there for another thirteen years in which he called people to the pure monotheistic belief of Islam. He then migrated to Madinah, and stayed there for ten years. He continued to receive revelation there, until the Qur'an and the religion of Islam were complete.

MUHAMMAD The Messenger of Allah

The famous playwright and critic, George Bernard Shaw (d. 1950) said:

"I have always held the religion of Muhammad in high estimation because of its wonderful vitality. It is the only religion which appears to possess that assimilating capability to the changing phases of existence which make itself appeal to every age. I have prophesized about the faith of Muhammad that it would be acceptable tomorrow as it is beginning to be acceptable to the Europe of today. Medieval ecclesiastics, either through ignorance or bigotry, painted [Islam] in the darkest colours. They were, in fact, trained to hate both the man Muhammad and his religion. To them, Muhammad was an anti-Christ. I have studied him, the wonderful man, and in my opinion, far from being an anti-Christ, he must be called the Saviour of Humanity."[1].

(1) George Bernard Shaw, "A Shavian Meets a Theologian" Interview by M A A Siddiqui in "Genuine Islam", Organ of the Al-Malaya Missionary Society Vol 1, No 1, January, 1936 B Lib catalogue

2

The Description of the Prophet ﷺ

From the book, *Shamaa'il At-Tirmidhî*, we learn that the Prophet ﷺ, as described by his Companion Anas b. Malik, was "neither very tall, such that he would be clearly noticed, nor was he short. He was not extremely white and neither was he very brown. His hair was neither very curly nor completely straight". Sometimes he would part his hair in the middle. Other times, he would wear it braided. The Prophet ﷺ had the physique of a powerful man. He had a broad upper-back and shoulders between which was the Seal of Prophethood mark. He had long muscular limbs with large joints. His lean stomach never protruded out past the profile of his chest. His face was radiant, **"as if the sun were following its course**

• Muhammad ﷺ

across and shining from his face," said one Companion. His forehead, prominent, his pupils, large and black, his eyelashes, long and thick, his nose, hightipped with narrow nostrils.

The Prophet would walk briskly with a forward leaning gait, moving with strength of purpose and lifting each foot clearly off the ground. His pace was such that fit men would tire trying to keep up. When he turned, he would turn his whole body, giving full attention to the one addressing him and showing complete concern to what was being said. When he pointed, he would use an open hand so as not to offend. Likewise, when he criticized a person's behavior, rather than name the individual, he would simply say, **"Why do people do such and such?"**

- May God highly praise Muhammad.

He would smile quite often, but his laugh was usually a measured one, generally only to the extent that his front teeth would become visible. He would become angry only to the extent that his face would turn red and the vein between his eyebrows would bulge.

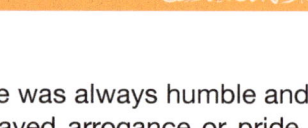

He was always humble and never displayed arrogance or pride. That freedom from pride was obvious even to children, who would playfully lead the Prophet ﷺ through the streets of Madinah whilst grasping his finger. Indeed, he had said:

"He who does not show mercy to our young, nor honor our old, is not from us." (Abu Dawood)

"[He sent] a Messenger [Muhammad] reciting to you the distinct verses of Allah that He may bring out those who believe and do righteous deeds from the darknesses into the light. And whoever believes in Allah and does righteousness - He will admit him into gardens beneath which rivers flow to abide therein forever. Allah will have perfected for him a provision." *[65:11]*

Ali, cousin and son-in-law to the Prophet ﷺ, said of Muhammad:

"He was the Last of the Prophets, the most giving of hearts, the most truthful, the best of them in temperament and the most sociable. Whoever unexpectedly saw him would stand in awe of him,

and whoever accompanied him and got to know him would love him. Those describing him would say, **'I have never seen anyone before or after him who was comparable to him.'"**

The Prophet's beloved wife, A'ishah, said of her selfless husband:

"He always joined in household chores and would at times mend his clothes, repair his shoes and sweep the floor. He would milk, tether and feed his animals." (Bukhari)

She was also once asked to describe his character, and she replied, **"His character was the Qur'an (exemplified)."** (Muslim)

"There has certainly been for you in the Messenger of Allah an excellent pattern for anyone whose hope is in Allah and the Last Day and [who] remembers Allah often." *[33:21]*

It is time to know Him
Rasoulallah.net

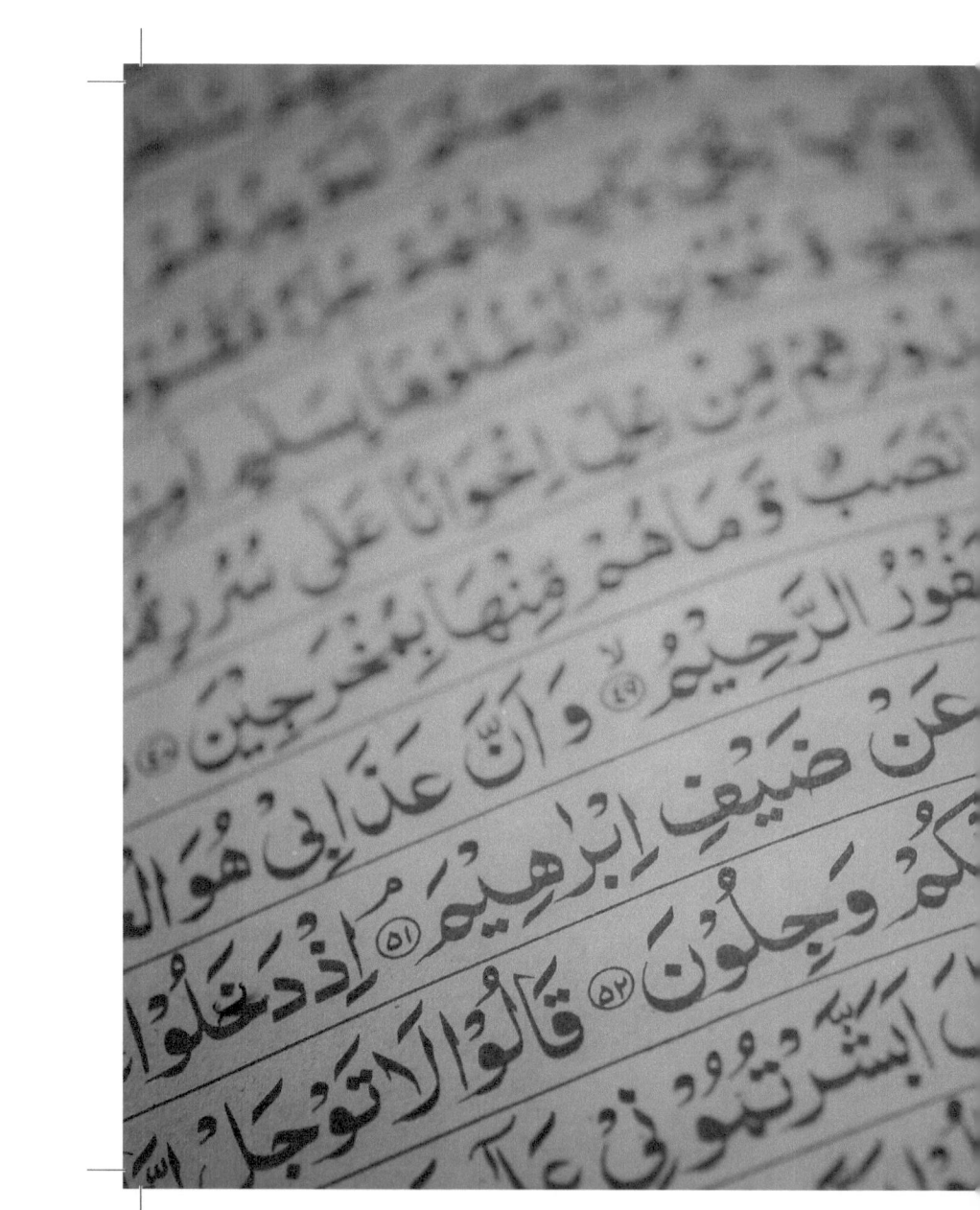

This booklet is the second in a series of publications based on a book titled **Muhammad, the Messenger of Allah**. Each booklet covers an aspect of the Prophet's life, deeds and teachings, and aims to provide a better understanding of Islam.

His Lineage, Childhood and Prophethood 01
Persecution and Hijra 02
His Manners & Characteristics 03
The Prophet's Manners With Those Around Him 04
Textual, Scriptural and Intellectual Testimonials of his Prophethood 05
Intellectual Proofs of his Prophethood 06
The Relevance of his Prophethood 07

www.ingramcontent.com/pod-product-compliance
Lightning Source LLC
LaVergne TN
LVHW070436080526
838202LV00034B/2654